Indian Americans

Nichol Bryan

ONE NATION

ABDO
Publishing Company

visit us at
www.abdopub.com

Published by ABDO Publishing Company, 4940 Viking Drive, Edina, Minnesota 55435.
Copyright © 2004 by Abdo Consulting Group, Inc. International copyrights reserved in all
countries. No part of this book may be reproduced in any form without written permission from
the publisher.

Printed in the United States.

Cover Photo: Corbis
Interior Photos: AP/Wide World p. 25; Corbis pp. 1, 2-3, 6, 7, 11, 15, 19, 22, 26, 30-31;
   Getty pp. 5, 9, 17, 28, 29; TimePix pp. 12, 21, 27

Editors: Kate A. Conley, Jennifer R. Krueger, Kristin Van Cleaf
Art Direction & Maps: Neil Klinepier

All of the U.S. population statistics in the One Nation series are taken from the 2000 Census.

Library of Congress Cataloging-in-Publication Data

Bryan, Nichol, 1958-
    Indian Americans / Nichol Bryan.
        p. cm. -- (One nation)
    Summary: Provides an overview of the life and culture of East Indian Americans and presents
some information on India.
    Includes bibliographical references and index.
    ISBN 1-57765-984-8
    1. East Indian Americans--Juvenile literature. [1. East Indian Americans. 2. Immigrants.]
    I. Title.

E184.E2B78 2003
973'.0491411--dc21

                                                                        2002043630

Contents

Indian Americans

India is a land in southern Asia, north of the Indian Ocean. The country is about one-third the size of the United States, but more than 1 billion people live there. The people are of a variety of religions and **ethnic** groups. They speak many languages.

The main wave of Indian **immigration** to the United States began just before 1900. Like many immigrants, Indians encountered **discrimination** and even hatred in the United States. Some left, but others remained. As time went on, attitudes in the United States changed. Indians started coming to the United States once again.

Today, Indian immigrants and their descendants are a part of American society. Many still follow their traditional **customs**. But, many Indian Americans have also changed as they have become a part of the United States. Their new homeland has changed along with them.

Opposite page: Sikh children wave American flags at a rally against discrimination.

An Ancient Culture

India is home to ancient **cultures**. The first cities in India were built more than 4,000 years ago! Over the centuries, the land has seen kingdoms come and go. Throughout that time, the Indian people created music, art, literature, and a strong tradition.

Western nations began occasionally trading with India in the 300s B.C. Over time, the Ottoman Empire blocked the land routes from western Europe to India. Then in A.D. 1498, Portuguese navigator Vasco da Gama sailed from Portugal to India. Trade was reestablished, bringing many other European countries back in contact with India.

Vasco da Gama

Mohandas Gandhi

India was a land known for its spices, silks, and exotic **culture**. Because of this, Western nations competed to trade goods with India. The British and the French fought for control of India in the mid-1700s. By the late 1700s, the British had begun taking over India.

In 1857, Indians **rebelled** against the British. The British maintained control of India, but they did make some government reforms. Many Indians banded together to support self-government, but it was slow in coming. At the same time, India faced other problems. India's Hindus and Muslims were constantly fighting over religion.

As conditions worsened, Indians began protesting. One of the most influential leaders was a man named Mohandas Gandhi. His nonviolent protests helped to finally free India from British rule in August 1947. At the same time, northern India became a separate Muslim country called Pakistan. Officials hoped this would reduce fighting between the Hindus and Muslims.

After independence, millions of Indians began to move. Many Hindus and Sikhs who found themselves living in the newly formed Pakistan fled to India. Likewise, many Muslims who found themselves living in India moved to Pakistan. Other Indians began **immigrating** to the United States.

As time passed, problems continued to plague India. India has had many conflicts with its neighbors. It has fought Pakistan, as well as China and Nepal. Inside India, different political parties continue to disagree, sometimes resulting in violence.

India faces other problems, too. **Monsoons** affect the weather every year. During some monsoon seasons, lots of rain falls. This sometimes leads to flooding, which destroys crops and homes. But in other seasons, there may be no rain at all, leading to droughts. In addition, tropical cyclones and earthquakes threaten injury and damage every year.

The regular monsoons can cause either flooding or drought. This lake in India dried up from lack of rain.

India also deals with a population problem. It has one of the biggest populations of any country. Experts think India will be home to 1.6 billion people by the middle of the twenty-first century! Though India is a big country, this large population makes it very crowded. In large cities such as Mumbai and Delhi, thousands of people are packed into crowded housing.

The Journey from India to the United States

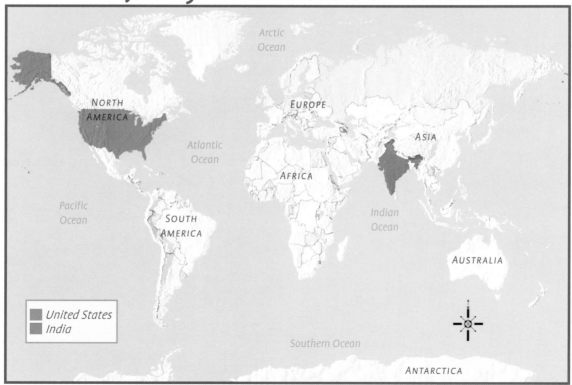

India's large population also creates the need for many resources, which are often scarce. For example, clean drinking water is hard to find, and the food supply depends on the **monsoon** season. Though some Indians are wealthy and well educated, many people are poor and hungry. Millions of them cannot get good health care, and diseases kill many Indians, especially children.

As a result, many Indians have recently left the hardships of their native country and **immigrated** to the United States. The United States has been considered a land of freedom and opportunity for hundreds of years. Still, immigrating has its challenges.

Indian children ride to school.

Coming to America

The first **immigrant** from India probably arrived in North America in 1790. For the next hundred years, however, few Indians moved to the United States. Hindu beliefs discouraged people from making the journey. In addition, British control of India kept many people from leaving. From 1820 to 1898, only about 520 Indians migrated to the United States.

Many of America's first Indian immigrants followed the Sikh religion. They came from Punjab, a region in India. They had been farmers in India, but land was scarce there, so they began looking for new opportunities. They first traveled to Canada and eventually settled in Washington, Oregon, and California. Most became farmers or industry laborers. Their wages were low, but they earned more money than they would have in India.

A Sikh immigrant studies bees in 1937.

By 1900, only about 2,000 Indian Americans lived in the United States. Those numbers began to increase, however, in the early 1900s. More Indian laborers saw that there was work in the United States. Between 1899 and 1913, several thousand Indians came to

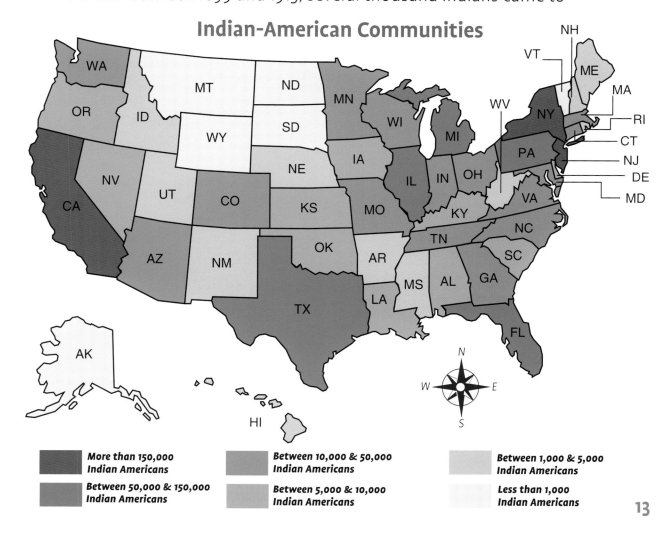

Indian-American Communities

work along the Pacific Coast. Soon, people began to worry that Indian Americans were taking jobs from other Americans. As a result, Indian Americans began to face **discrimination**.

Anti-**immigration** groups encouraged discrimination against Indians and other immigrants. Soon, Indians were not allowed to enter the country with their families or to become citizens. In addition, gangs of white men sometimes attacked Indian farm laborers. Nearly 700 Indians fled to Canada and elsewhere to escape this hatred. In 1914, little more than a hundred Indians immigrated. Soon, they were not allowed to enter the United States at all.

By 1940, only about 2,400 Indian Americans lived in the United States. Then in 1946, a bill was signed. It included a **quota** allowing 100 Indians to enter the country every year. It also allowed Indians to become U.S. citizens. In 1952, the quota was changed, and entire Indian families were allowed to enter the United States.

Slowly, the Indian-American community began to grow. Between 1948 and 1965, more than 6,000 Indians entered the United States. Indian neighborhoods began to grow and take on a more Indian atmosphere. Indian women often wore their native dresses. Sikh men sometimes wore turbans. In places such as California, Sikhs and others built beautiful new temples.

A boy studies at a Sikh temple in New Jersey.

When the **quotas** ended in the 1960s, more Indian **immigrants** arrived. These immigrants were not poor farmers. Rather, they were educated and skilled people looking for opportunity.

Since the **terrorist** attacks of September 11, 2001, Indian Americans face a new problem. Some Indian Americans have a skin color similar to that of the Middle Easterners who carried out the terrorist attacks. This makes Indian Americans subject to the same **discrimination** and fear that is directed at Middle Easterners.

As a result, Indian Americans are often stopped and searched in airports and are the victims of discrimination and violence. Sikhs, who wear turbans for religious reasons, draw the most suspicion. Their turbans make people think they are from the Middle East. Though most Middle Easterners are not terrorists, some people still fear that Middle Easterners may have connections to terrorism.

Still, not every American feels this way. Many have shown support for their Indian-American neighbors. Today, nearly 1.6 million Americans are of Indian descent. They form a part of modern American society, while still blending some Indian traditions into their lives. They hope to help America continue its tradition of **cultural** diversity.

More than 1 million Americans have some Indian heritage.

Becoming a Citizen

Indians and other **immigrants** who come to the United States take the same path to citizenship. Immigrants become citizens in a process called naturalization. A government agency called the Immigration and Naturalization Service (INS) oversees this process.

The Path to Citizenship

Applying for Citizenship

The first step in becoming a citizen is filling out a form. It is called the Application for Naturalization. On the application, immigrants provide information about their past. Immigrants send the application to the INS.

Providing Information

Besides the application, immigrants must provide the INS with other items. They may include documents such as marriage licenses or old tax returns. Immigrants must also provide photographs and fingerprints. They are used for identification. The fingerprints are also used to check whether immigrants have committed crimes in the past.

The Interview

Next, an INS officer interviews each immigrant to discuss his or her application and background. In addition, the INS officer tests the immigrant's ability to speak, read, and write in English. The officer also tests the immigrant's knowledge of American civics.

The Oath

Immigrants approved for citizenship must take the Oath of Allegiance. Once immigrants take this oath, they are citizens. During the oath, immigrants promise to renounce loyalty to their native country, to support the U.S. Constitution, and to serve and defend the United States when needed.

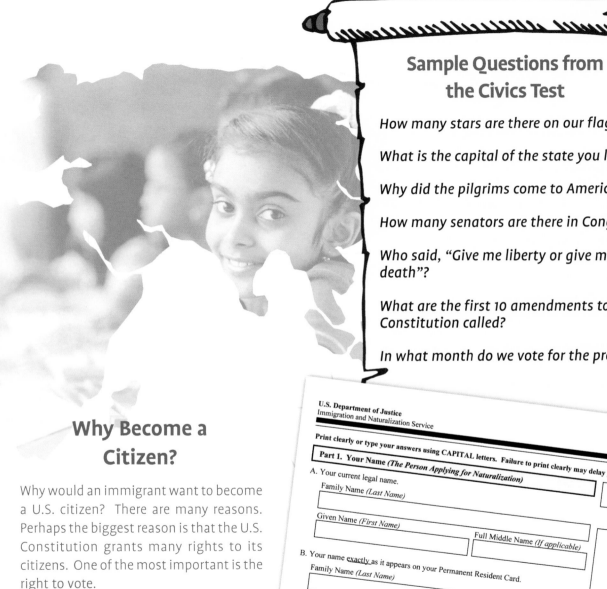

Sample Questions from the Civics Test

How many stars are there on our flag?

What is the capital of the state you live in?

Why did the pilgrims come to America?

How many senators are there in Congress?

Who said, "Give me liberty or give me death"?

What are the first 10 amendments to the Constitution called?

In what month do we vote for the president?

Why Become a Citizen?

Why would an immigrant want to become a U.S. citizen? There are many reasons. Perhaps the biggest reason is that the U.S. Constitution grants many rights to its citizens. One of the most important is the right to vote.

U.S. Department of Justice
Immigration and Naturalization Service

Print clearly or type your answers using CAPITAL letters. Failure to print clearly may delay your application. Use bl

Application f

Part 1. Your Name *(The Person Applying for Naturalization)*

A. Your current legal name.

Family Name *(Last Name)*

Write your INS "A"- n

A _ _ _ _ _ _

Given Name *(First Name)*

Full Middle Name *(If applicable)*

FOR INS U

Bar Code

B. Your name <u>exactly</u> as it appears on your Permanent Resident Card.

Family Name *(Last Name)*

Given Name *(First Name)*

Full Middle Name *(If applicable)*

C. If you have ever used other names, provide them below.

Family Name *(Last Name)*

Given Name *(First Name)*

Middle Name

Traditional Ways

Indians are a people who care about tradition. Although some of their **customs** have changed in America, Indian Americans are still careful to follow many of the traditions they followed in India. They pass these traditions down to their children.

Family

Indian-American families are similar to most other American families. Parents and children live together, and extended family may often come to visit. Once settled in the United States, many Indian Americans encourage family members who are still in India to **emigrate**. Often, Indian Americans help support recent **immigrants** until they are settled. Indian Americans believe it is their duty to look after their family members.

Indian families are often very traditional. The husband works while the wife cares for the children and house. Today, however, Indian-American women tend to have more freedom to choose what they will do. Many have decided to have careers outside of their homes.

Indian Ways

For many Indian Americans, following **customs** is important. That may mean being part of an arranged marriage. Parents often find a wife or husband for their son or daughter. They look at a person's education, religious views, interests, and social **caste**. They hope that matching interests will lead to a happy marriage. However, this is a custom that is changing in America.

An Indian-American shopkeeper and his son stand in their sari clothing store.

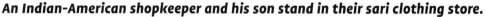

Indian restaurants have become popular in many American cities.

Another **custom** some Indian Americans follow is wearing traditional clothing. Though Indian Americans often wear Western-style clothes, some choose to wear clothing from their native land. Some women wear a sari. This garment is a long cloth wrapped as an ankle-length skirt and draped over one shoulder. Most saris are very colorful and can be made of cotton or fine embroidered silks.

Spicy Treats

Indian food has also made its way to America. Vegetables, rice, lentils, and grains are just a few main ingredients used in Indian cooking. Many kinds of spices add flavor, and some can be quite hot! A common food is curry, which is a sauce made from a blend of spices. Yogurt and fruit are also often served in Indian meals.

Indian meals often reflect religious beliefs. For example, many Indians who follow the Hindu religion are vegetarians. In addition, Muslims do not eat pork. Indians have created many tasty vegetarian meals because of this. Some Indians born in the United States, however, decide not to be vegetarians.

Celebrations

Diwali is a Hindu festival celebrated in October. This festival of light is celebrated by Hindus around the world. For the festival, Hindus light small oil lamps and make offerings to Hindu gods. Many Indian Americans also celebrate with Indian music and dancing. Dancers dress in beautiful clothing and jewelry.

A Land of Many Tongues

India is a land of many languages. In fact, nearly 300 different dialects are spoken there. Hindi is the national language and one of the 15 official languages. English is also one of the official languages, because Britain influenced India for more than 100 years.

Because so many Indians today know at least some English, they have an easier time after arriving in the United States. New arrivals often speak their native language at home or with relatives. Descendants of **immigrants** can often understand the language of their parents or grandparents, but they cannot always speak it.

Hinduism & Other Faiths

As in India, most Indian Americans follow the Hindu faith. Hindus believe that after a person dies, his or her soul is reborn. The soul can be reborn as a person or even an animal. How a person is reborn depends on karma, the result of the good and evil things done in a previous life. By doing good works, performing rituals, and meditating, Hindus believe a person can break free of the endless cycle of birth and death.

The Hindu faith also honors many gods. One god is Vishnu, who created the universe by separating heaven and earth. Another god is Ganesha, who has the head of an elephant. Many Hindus pray to Ganesha for good luck and success.

Not all Indian Americans are Hindu. Some Indian Americans who **emigrated** from northern India follow Islam. In addition, Sikhs practice a religion related to both Hinduism and Islam. Indian Americans may also be Jain, Buddhist, or Christian.

An Indian-American child explores a Hindu temple in Pennsylvania.

25

Contributions

Indians who moved to the United States brought a **culture** devoted to music, art, philosophy, mathematics, and science. So, it's no surprise that Indian Americans have made important contributions in all these fields.

Many Indian Americans are leaders in technology. For instance, many of today's computers would not work without the Pentium processor chip created by Vinod Dham. Dham's work on the processor earned him the nickname "Father of the Pentium."

Indian-American technical expertise goes beyond computers. The famous Bose speaker system is the invention of Amar Bose, an Indian American. NASA's Chandra X-ray Observatory is named in honor

Subrahmanyan Chandrasekhar

of the late Subrahmanyan Chandrasekhar. This Indian American was one of the greatest astrophysicists of the twentieth century. In 1983, he won the Nobel Prize in physics.

Indian Americans have also been leaders in the world of entertainment. Ravi Shankar gained notice during the 1960s. He plays the sitar, a traditional instrument in Indian classical music. This world-renowned musician helped make Indian music popular in the United States. He was even a major influence on the Beatles! Shankar's influence can especially be heard in the Beatles song "Within You, Without You."

Ravi Shankar performs a piece of Indian music on his sitar.

One of Shankar's daughters, Norah Jones, is a second-generation Indian American who has become a celebrity in her own right. She was born in New York and grew up in Texas. She became interested in jazz music while still in high school. In 2002, her recording of the song "Don't Know Why" became a major hit in the United States.

Indian Americans have also written best-selling books. Bharati Mukherjee is an Indian-American writer who was born in Kolkata. She lived in England and Canada before coming to the United States. Mukherjee writes about the problems of **immigrants** and their fight to maintain their **heritage** in a new society. Her book *The Middleman and Other Stories* won an award from the National Book Critics Circle in 1988.

Another respected Indian American in the arts is film producer Ismail Merchant. He developed a love of movies while he was a child in Mumbai. After coming to the United States, he met James Ivory, a filmmaker from California. They began working together, and their company has produced more than 30 movies. Two of their most popular films are *Howards End* and *A Room With a View*.

Ismail Merchant at a book signing

Kalpana Chawla was a respected astronaut who was born in India. Her passion for flying led her to study **aeronautics** in both India and the United States. She eventually became a U.S. citizen, and in 1994, an astronaut. In 1997, she became the first Indian-born woman in space. She was serving as Flight Engineer and Mission Specialist 2 on the *Columbia* when it broke into pieces as it was returning to Earth in February 2003.

About traveling in space, Chawla once said, "The earth is very beautiful. I wish everyone could see it."

Although India is a poor country, its children have inherited a beautiful **culture**. Indian Americans have held on to many of their culture's traditions, even after coming to America. They are making all Americans richer by sharing that culture.

Glossary

aeronautics - the science that studies flight and the operation of aircraft.

caste - a social class based on wealth, profession, or occupation.

culture - the customs, arts, and tools of a nation or people at a certain time.

customs - the habits of a group that are passed on through generations.

discrimination - unfair treatment based on factors such as a person's race, religion, or gender.

emigration - to leave one's country and move to another. People who emigrate are called emigrants.

ethnic - of or having to do with a group of people who have the same race, nationality, or culture.

heritage - the handing down of something from one generation to the next.

immigration - entry into another country to live. People who immigrate are called immigrants.

monsoon - a season of wind that sometimes brings heavy rains.

quota - a limit to the number of people allowed to immigrate in a year. Immigration quotas are based on where a person is from.

rebel - to disobey an authority or the government.

terrorism - the use of terror, threats, or violence to frighten people into action. A person who terrorizes is called a terrorist.

Saying It

Bharti Mukherjee - BAH-ruh-tee MOOK-er-jee
Ismail Merchant - IS-may-ehl MUR-chuhnt
Kalpana Chawla - KUHL-puh-nah CHAO-lah
Mohandas Gandhi - moh-huhn-DAHS GAHN-dee
Ravi Shankar - RAHV-ee SHANK-ahr
Sikh - SEEK
Subrahmanyan Chandrasekhar - suh-brah-MAN-yuhn chuhn-druh-SHAY-kahr

Web Sites

To learn more about Indian Americans, visit ABDO Publishing
Company on the World Wide Web at **www.abdopub.com**. Web sites
about Indian life in America are featured on our Book Links page.
These links are routinely monitored and updated to provide the
most current information available.

31

Index